GRACE

A Sacred Journey

DAWN CUMMINS

GRACE
A Sacred Journey

First published in 2021 by
Panoma Press Ltd
48 St Vincent Drive, St Albans, Herts, AL1 5SJ UK

info@panomapress.com
www.panomapress.com

Cover design and book layout by Angie Phillips

ISBN 978-1-784529-40-6

This book is available online and in all good bookstores.

DEDICATION

*To all Awakening Hearts, who
are now ready for their own
unique Sacred Journey of the soul,
through the power of prayer called
GRACE, which is the glory of
God.
We are and have entered into the
2021 Aquarian universal energy,
the awakening of the dawning, the
dawning of the age of Aquarius.*

TESTIMONIALS

In a beautifully eloquent way, Dawn walks the reader through the teachings of the heart. She illuminates the 'Sacred Journey' our souls take towards the wisdom of our oneness with God, offering insights to assist us to be who we truly are right now! GRACE is a book full of compassion, integrity, faith and wisdom, all much needed in these times. Enjoy!

Emma Robinson, Reiki Master/Shamanic Healer

Dawn, the Inspirational Author has created a tool that needs to be used in everyone's daily life and it should be the new Bible. This magical book has the power to activate the love and the truth that every being holds within and also makes you feel connected on a deeper level, feeling clarified to what life and the Grace of God is all about. I hope everyone is lucky enough to read this blessing of a book.

Eleanor Jayne Bloomfield, Spiritual Digital Creator

Being a Buddhist my understanding of God is different from Dawn's and probably to you the reader. So I was naturally hesitant to read Dawn's wonderful book. But once I got out of my own way and opened my heart to accept a different view of God/The Source/ Universe, I was filled with a sense of compassion, hope and strength, coming from Dawn's words, and boy don't we need it right now. Whatever your religion, your views or beliefs, this book will be a welcome guide on your journey. Go well fellow travellers.

Chris Croucher, Quest for the Green Man

CONTENTS

ACKNOWLEDGMENTS

I am forever grateful to many individual souls who have surrounded and supported me on my own Sacred Journey. Helping with the realisation that my life purpose is communication, to becoming a Transformational/Spiritual Author and truly connecting with the voice of my soul. You have all contributed in so many different and loving ways, I thank you all. I am also thankful to the Grace of God, and to many non-physical beings who work with and through me.

OPENING PRAYER

Greet the Dawn

That is your miracle to witness
That is the ultimate beauty
That is sacredness
That is your gift from heaven
That is your omen of prophecy
That is knowledge that life is not futile
That is enlightenment
That is your meaning of life
That is your directive
That is your comfort
That is the solemnity of duty
That is inspiration for compassion
That is the light of the ultimate

INTRODUCTION

THE TRILOGY:
GRACE – A SACRED JOURNEY

In 2014, I wrote my first book with a strong desire to share a divine Message of Love, in fact this is the title of the book. Three years later in 2017, my second book with the continuation of the divine message, Invisible Wings. The Power of Invisibility was ready to come into alignment with God's divine plan. The content of this book had been in my psyche for a while, I knew I had wanted to write about Invisibility for a long time, but I didn't understand it enough then to write about it.

Intuitively I had this passion and love for life, and God was at that time guiding me to share my message of love, my journey/ story with the world, to inspire and uplift others who, like me, were ready to help themselves too.

So from doing that, it led me to then having the awareness, clarity and confirmation that one day I knew I would write a book about Invisibility, and I had that epiphany one day as I was travelling back from London on the train to understanding why Invisibility was going to be a crucial part of who I was to become.

The realisation of writing my books was going to be a huge healing transformation on my personal and spiritual development journey, and that continuation of my journey has now brought me again to the divine timing, such times where many are also experiencing this perfect timing, it truly is in alignment with the Now.

Jesus, please guide my words and actions to reflect your true message. Help me mirror your love to everyone I meet.

I am bringing good news, I present to you my third book which is so ready to be presented to the world, and I so love divine timing. I am excited about celebrating this trilogy of my three books coming together, into the flow of this global activity of 2021 where we are experiencing a true solid connection of who we all are.

It is a constant cosmic flow in a year of completion. Showing that spirituality is normal, so embrace it, own it, be it. We are embarking on a period where humanity is creating this new understanding of who God is.

The alignment of this truly wonderful Aquarian universal five-energy year [awareness, acceptance, inner freedom] is time to embrace this fifth-dimensional life, the sacred awakening of the heart, releasing an ego-based consciousness. Ready to grow towards a heart-centred consciousness, connecting to the Christ Consciousness.

This process of transformation is what many people are now experiencing, understanding and realising that the world is changing. Knowing that their spiritual awakening is that journey from within.

Releasing external negativity, guiding you to get to the core of yourself, and within that core you are Spirit. When you get to that place, then you will experience a deep sense of relief, peace, reclaiming your power, with grace and ease.

The ultimate message for my books has been about love, supporting and encouraging all souls who were, and are, ready to embrace the love of self as they go through their own Personal Transformation. Also beginning to want to understand about Sensitivity, Vulnerability and Invisibility, and their own inner support system.

The first chapter in my first book was "God is Love" – this is over six years ago now, it felt brave to write about God. In many ways I was ready, I felt it was for my own growth. I really did want to share that deeper feeling that I was experiencing, because the truth personally was at that stage for my own healing. The importance of trusting my own understanding of the inner work was needed to become more confident in believing God is love. Not only for myself but for everyone, that God is inside of us all and all things really do come to the light.

That light led me and guided me on an incredible Sacred Journey of feeling worthy of God's grace, truly knowing God's love is inside of me. I know from that deep place in my heart that my third book is going to be an introduction to you and so many souls who are now ready for the same experience, wanting to embrace this powerful feeling of the Christ Consciousness connection.

This will guide you to find the true meaning of this Sacred Journey of the soul you are now finding yourself on. Allowing your empathic sensitive nature to return from the Grace of God, to living this divine message of love.

This book is also such a testament to those who might be ready to want to understand more about the Bible. GRACE – A Sacred Journey is a book that can make you feel like you have a Bible, feeling inspired and wanting to read it every day, or just hold it and randomly open it and read what you see. Believe me you will feel the presence of God's love, it's a powerful and beautiful experience.

I want to say and share with you that my experience with the Bible has not been easy. If there ever was an excuse, mine was that the print was too small, an excuse that I found myself procrastinating with for much too long. So when a Bible class became available, it got my attention. It was and felt the perfect time, I felt God guiding me to do it.

I knew I was ready to find out for myself if it was going to help me. What I did learn was that you could buy Bibles that have larger print, also about an app that is available on a mobile phone, called YouVersion. This made it so much easier and more accessible to read. I made a good attempt in reading it this way and I now quote the Bible a lot more, as the scriptures are important to me.

So a very positive outcome from joining the Bible class, where I do now find reading the Bible a lot easier, and how I now understand the glory of God. Having learned so much also encouraged me to want to share the word of God.

How the sacredness of the tri-unity of the journey, our God is three in one – God the Father, Jesus the Son and the Holy Spirit – showed me the aspect and understanding of the trilogy, meaning the magic three of my books coming together.

The divine trilogy of the number 3 reminds you of your ability to co-create with the Divine, as in the Divine Trinity, therefore the number that is repeated three times is a wake-up call to your creative manifesting powers.

To illustrate the magical creative power of the number 3, let's just look at the miracle of birth, in which two people can create a third being. You have that power of creation within you every day, giving birth to new ideas, nurturing seeds you may have sown, whether thought forms, or any physical manifestation that you desire. The number 3 reminds you to express yourself in many ways, sharing what's in your heart, to express your unique voice.

It is a sensitive, expressive vibration, also reminding you to honour your emotions, tune into your feelings, psyche and soul.

This is the number of pure joy, because you will feel so much joy when speaking your truth, expressing your creativity, which I have now allowed myself to do.

A truly heavenly reminder that you are more than enough right now. Love yourself for who you are, keep embracing the divine message from God to be yourself.

Let this book of GRACE – A Sacred Journey be the next chapter in your life inspiring you to really want to read it daily, just like an introduction to the Bible. It will be a powerful experience of connecting with the tri-unity.

God who creates and loves us, Jesus for his salvation, friendship and abundant life, and the Holy Spirit, enlightening, guiding, transforming us today and every day. Truly demonstrating God is love, to really trusting, believing and having faith.

Yes, God is in charge, put him first always, I know and believe it was part of his plan for me to write my three books, sharing the message, the word of God, encouraging everyone to be inspired.

Surrender, gain God confidence, you don't have to do this alone, ask for his strength and support for what steps to take. He does hear your prayers, his law is love and his Gospel is peace.

God help us to find a place of your grace, lead and guide us with your grace and teach me how to walk in your glory.

This is the gift of his Holy Presence.

PREFACE

A Sacred Journey
Sacred Love

What is a Sacred Journey, what defines a Sacred Journey?

Most commonly, it would be a pilgrimage, a sacred place and very often part of a spiritual journey, connecting to a higher love, a sacred love. They say the backbone of a Sacred Journey is actually the pain of the journey itself.

A Sacred Journey – two words that are quite different, but they can have an emphasis on your spiritual path and personal growth. A journey can be defined for those who decide to travel with an intention of undertaking spiritual practices, to where they will attain, succeed and achieve what they have worked and aimed for in regards to their spiritual growth.

This could mean involving participation in both religious and non-religious activities, as everyone will have their own views, because the word sacred will mean different things to the individual person.

My belief is we are born sacred, and personally the word sacred feels very special. It has such depth, it is meaningful, a love that is pure and gentle, that perfect calming energy where you always feel supported and guided by God's love, having faith in his word and him helping you activate his glory.

We are not in control or in charge, God is in charge, he created all things because of love, so everything he created is sacred, allowing us to stay open to receive everything that is holy and sacred.

"Oh Sacred Heart please come to me, as I want to be free, embracing God's glory, holy, holy, holy. Breathing in his strength, goodness and peace, feeling his presence, and feeling holy, holy, holy."

A true sacred connection with God is holy, simply worthy of awe and deserving of respect. Sacred can be anything worthy of worship, and sometimes it is used to describe a person, and declared as holy.

It is important and highly recommended to create and find your own sacred space, creating calm and honouring your power. Spirituality and intention are sacred, vital in helping you become more disciplined and devoted in your own spiritual practice, to then finding that balance and feeling grounded.

When you hear others talk about sacred gifts, what does that mean to you? What comes to mind? Because I feel all of God's gifts are sacred.

Whether you worship in a church or worship outside in nature, to overlooking the beautiful ocean. I know for myself the ocean is where I feel connected to God, but equally they are all sacred and gifts individually.

Personally there have been so many other special gifts that I can now understand, and why they have been instrumental on my transformational journey. Sensitivity, Vulnerability and Invisibility were three of them, and it took me some time to really embrace them, because I believed they were weaknesses. But even then they became and still are such positive parts of who I am.

I found my understanding of these gifts/lessons truly did connect me with the thread of love and light, knowing that we can all receive that gift for our self, which is unconditional love.

My beliefs are that I was born with these special gifts that were going to be part of my life lessons, being sensitive and vulnerable were very present from birth into my childhood.

Of course, I didn't know then they were to become such strengths, and very much later on was when the gift of Invisibility became not only my friend but a strength that helped me become who I truly am. These three gifts of Sensitivity, Vulnerability and Invisibility were so special and sacred to me on my journey.

So what do I see when I think of a Sacred Heart? I see this glowing golden light, I feel compassion and see it filled with unconditional love, caring and joyful too.

My Sacred Journey unfolded as I went within, learning that being sensitive and vulnerable could really be my strengths, which was no surprise either because I am an introvert, and Invisibility was showing me how I could balance being invisible and visible when needed. So the weaknesses that I believed I had were what I had allowed society to demonstrate them to be.

The sacredness of many other beautiful things will include human life, temples, scriptures and writings for instance, as all of them have a divine nature and destiny.

Temples are sacred, as are other buildings all dedicated to God, including those of worship. The scriptures, writings would have been given by God to persuade people.

Families and all our relationships have a certain amount of responsibility to love and care for each other, and parents would have that deep "sacred duty" in raising their children.

So what is the journey, what does it mean when you hear it said, I am on a journey? The word journey has become widely and worldly used to express something that we endure. Quite often you may hear some say the "J" word when a journey is brought up because it is a term used quite a lot. The Journey of Life is about our earthly lessons, and life is a journey not a destination, as every lesson or experience has no finish line, it is a supreme destiny, calling on your light.

Those lessons could be filled with hardships, heartaches, celebrations and special moments, ultimately they could eventually lead you to a destination, which becomes a purpose in life. But if you are not listening, you could come off track, because all your lessons are there to wake you up, helping you to create and put you on the right path, but also remember your daily life is the path.

There is no failure, as spiritually you are constantly unfolding and embracing all those forks in the road, with the bumps too. Keep reclaiming your spirituality, as somehow it feels like the true meaning has been lost over time.

So your daily path will not always run smoothly, in fact on or throughout your journey you will encounter challenges, but in reality it does express the journey perfectly, because that's what you do, you go on a journey.

The experience is something that takes you somewhere continuously in life, which is your life journey, and mistakes would never be a waste of time as nothing is lost. But it is about finding true beauty in all the breakdowns or situations that challenge you.

In and through your life journey, your soul's journey, you will experience transformation, as God does transformative work in us and the world. A process of that transformation and your personal development would express the journey you would experience with yourself.

Through my own personal development and spiritual transformation, it led me to become a Transformational Spiritual Author. Helping myself was always a strength, changing to then wanting to help others help themselves.

Helping others and encouraging them to become more comfortable with talking spiritually, embracing and supporting their own journey was also important. Expressing how spending quality time daily in quiet contemplation, and using the space which they could create for themselves.

Can you remember that sacred space I mentioned earlier? Where you allow yourself to get into an elevated state. Emotionally this will also help stimulate your body's immune system, as stress has been known to weaken our immune system.

So it is crucial to find ways to become calmer and really nurture yourself, as your body can then do what it would naturally do, self-regulate and self-heal, allowing you to then find that you will begin to discover mysteries as you explore your inner journey, and not so much from the outer part of your journey.

Finding Grace

"A little ray of sunshine, a smile sent from God, the start of a new journey, on a path that is well trod.

In some ways a reflection, in others fresh and new, reminders of a presence and a love that's oh so true.

So now begins the story, new dreams and tales to tell, both familiar and hopeful, and thoughts of wishing well.

Adventures will await you and challenges you'll face, a life of rediscovery… of joy and finding grace."

Robert Longley

God is known to be a great mystery, so you can learn to place your faith in him. Explore your inner world, your God self, it is all deep within you, as is all the knowledge of the Universe. You are connected to all of it, to Source/God, so just allow yourself to go within, becoming quiet and trust what you feel and what you find, trust your knowing. God is another name for Infinite Intelligence. So, to achieve anything in life, a piece of his intelligence must be contacted and used – in other words, God is always there for you.

The book *How to Know God* is written by Deepak Chopra, he shares these seven responses of the human brain, they are avenues to attain some aspect of God. The fulfilment of each level proves God's reality.

1. Fight or Flight Response. You fulfil your life through family, community, a sense of belonging and material comforts.

2. Reactive Response. You fulfil your life through success, power, influence, status and other ego satisfactions.

3. Restful Awareness Response. You fulfil your life through peace, centredness, self-acceptance and inner silence.

4. Intuitive Response. You fulfil your life through insight, empathy, tolerance and forgiveness.

5. Creative Response. You fulfil your life through inspiration, expanded creativity in art or science and unlimited discovery.

6. Visionary Response. You fulfil your life through reverence, compassion, devoted service and universal love.

7. Sacred Response. You fulfil your life through wholeness and unity with the Divine.

I like the 7th Sacred Response aspect, knowing it is where your life is whole and proving God's reality. Where having unity with the Divine is a special place to arrive in your life, it is also important to know that Spirit involves a constant process.

Then the unfolding mysteries of Spirit begin to make sense, but to manifest the power of the Holy Spirit and God's glory, you need to step out of your comfort zone, daring to do the impossible, and putting your trust in God.

Here is a good question to ask yourself:

"Am I breathing like God designed me to?"

Andy Elmes

A short sentence, but I think it really can and will make you think. I can actually say that I knew a good while back, and I thought to myself, honestly, I don't think I am. I decided, yes I wanted to understand more about am I breathing like God designed me to, knowing I am worthy of every breath.

How can you let go of striving to live an anxiety-free life, where being overwhelmed seems to trigger anxiousness, causing panic attacks and hyperventilation? Today's lifestyle that we have created seems to be the norm, in the lives of many. But anxiety and worry are not what God/Jesus wants for your life. Peace of mind and a state of inner health and wellbeing are.

God has your back, he really wants you to trade your anxiety and fears for his peace and rest. Surely being fearful, not breathing peacefully, which causes you to become anxious, is worth considering, and simply trusting and having faith in Jesus.

The message/feeling that I experienced was that I limit myself, ultimately limiting my full potential of the breath of life that God has given me. Through God and breathing naturally in and out, as he designed me to do, is such a sustainable and precious gift of life.

I am grateful for this profound but simple sentence that just might trigger you too, wanting to understand more. It may trigger something deeper inside yourself, your soul, to see what your life is really offering you.

Also it will give you a better understanding of balancing these two different words, Sacred Journey, knowing that your inner journey is sacred, and this is why I believe we are born sacred. To learn such heartfelt sacredness in our hearts, to learning and understanding not to look outside of ourselves for that love of self.

"There is a candle in your heart, ready to be rekindled. There is a void in your soul, ready to be filled. You feel it, don't you?"

Rumi

The inward journey is where you can learn to find that peace, feeling peaceful with ourselves and the world, projecting it outwardly for that transformation to unfold lovingly.

"You are a Divine Sovereign. Do you know what that means? Everything that you have been through was against all the odds to show you how powerful you truly are. Everything you have been through, dark vs light, was designed for you to finally understand your almighty greatness as a Sacred Divine Sovereign Being."

Divine Mother

I really feel this verse has that feeling of empowerment, and in so many ways makes a Sacred Journey worth travelling as it gives new direction and meaning.

Thank you God for empowering us all to live on a supernatural plane of your grace and abundance, we trust in you, we are forever grateful.

Your will be done.

CHAPTER 1

GRACE

THE GRACE OF GOD

A SACRED JOURNEY

GRACE

THE GRACE OF GOD

My desire is to share the grace in this book with you, the reader, and with the world.

Grace is such a beautiful name. It has been considered a classic name since 1910, also known to have been the 75th most popular girl's name. Grace Kelly the [actress] icon, has also been linked and partly thanked for helping it to be a feminine girl's name, that has a gentle and caring energy attached to it.

The name Grace would have also been heard and spoken quite often as it is used in reference to the Christian concept of divine grace. We are very blessed to have the Virtue of Grace, as it is a special gift, meaning gracious, and not just for ballerinas who express such gracefulness, but also known for its quality of being morally good, showing kindness and love.

The Biblical meaning in the New Testament quotes that grace is the English translation of the Greek [*charis*]. A love defined by grace, and a nurturing heart which brings delight, joy, happiness, and spiritually the name Grace also comes from the Christian and Greek culture, meaning love and the blessing of God.

"GOD is LOVE, GOD is GRACE

When I float on water, I vow to rest in God's grace."

So what does having grace mean, and what happens when you accept grace? The Circle of Grace is the physical link to your inner divine power, it allows you to feel at ease being part of the flow of energy and be in your true essence, because we know grace is present everywhere all of the time, whether we notice it or not, grace is working. Truly, it is a gift of God.

"For by grace are ye saved through faith, and that not of yourselves; it is the gift of God."

Ephesians 2: 8

That moment can be when you feel contentment, peace, feel connected and aligned to the Divine, experiencing grace, to knowing and reminding you that you are never alone or unsupported.

God is the Sovereign Author, Sovereign means God is in control of everything, his grace flows through us which allows this grace to flow also out into the world.

"Grace was against my will, till God's grace changed me to accept his grace."

John M. Sheehan

His grace does include giving us free will of our own choice, referring to the power or right of an individual, not controlled by others. Self-determination and freedom are bestowed on us by God, as both are said to be intrinsic rights. We would take full responsibility of our lives, which would include not falling into the "victim" mentality trap, getting caught up in the blame and complain game, as this is only going to give away our power.

We are Powerful Sovereign Beings, connecting to the energy of the Universe and it is time to start acting like it. This power holds your own deepest truth and always goes back to knowing how you are feeling inside.

Commanding your power is based upon the sure and steady knowledge that you are a part of the Great Spirit, grace and wisdom. It is your lightning rod that can conduct the power, simply connecting through the strength and clarity of your thought processes, knowing this natural power resides within you.

Reclaiming your personal power also starts with forming your own "beliefs", trusting your inner truth, knowledge, do and stand for what you know is right in your heart, regaining that power and not always what society expects, and not what others tell you.

My personal affirmation is:

"I made a decision to be true to myself and stop being a follower."

Grace empowers you, and once awakened you begin to feel this most precious and gracious connection, the Kingdom of God is inside of you.

"For thine is the power and glory, for ever and ever, amen."

Matthew 6: 13

Having the influence of grace is God operating in humans to strengthen and regenerate them, allowing grace to empower them, helping to bring back that quiet stillness of its power and presence, giving that warm embrace and connection of empowerment.

Making room and time for grace quietly reminds us of who we are to knowing there is a place for grace in our lives, because it is an ordinary everyday presence.

Have you ever thought of how songs can also have a meaningful impact on our life journey, supporting our wellbeing on a deep level of healing as singing is sacred and it is the voice of God?

For instance, the hymn Amazing Grace, I love this hymn. The words: "I once was lost but now I'm found" are a true reminder of my own spiritual transformation, as the words did fit my description of a lost identity, where I was on a very long, painful journey of finding myself. The hymn starts with:

"Amazing Grace! How sweet the sound that saved a wretch like me. I once was lost, but now I'm found, was blind but now I see. 'Twas grace that taught my heart to fear, and grace my fears relieved, how precious did that grace appear, the hour I first believed. Through many dangers, toils and snares, I have already come. 'Tis grace that brought me safe thus far and Grace will lead me home."

John Newton

My experience might help you love and understand yourself, because love, grace and intention are receiving, and the gift of grace has helped me find myself in so many positive and wonderful ways.

Believe you deserve and the Universe will serve. Do you feel worthy of God's love?

God always had a plan, did he say it would be easy? Oh no, as it would be all part of my life's lessons, as I continued on my journey of finding myself, really questioning myself too.

Here is a short insight into my spiritual transformation over the last 20-plus years in the hope it might resonate with you, helping in some way.

Born a quiet, shy, timid and sensitive child who experienced many childhood ailments like shingles, chickenpox, and extremely bad coughs which were all signs of having a sensitive immune and nervous system.

My early years spent at school were good and I enjoyed school then, and it was probably where I felt safe. But I feel and believe once I went into the next chapter of my life, from leaving primary to starting secondary school, would have been the start of losing myself, the loss of my identity, becoming a lost soul, as this experience can and is known to be quite disruptive and common in a child's life.

That memory can still be quite raw at times, as it was frightening and scary, but in this day it would now be identified or known as anxiety, and feeling vulnerable was an understatement.

When healing a lost identity, also a term would be known as misuse of your power and fear-based, also negative in a controlling way, as we can all tend to give our power away more often than not. What we would really need to achieve is to own it, feel empowered and be at one with our power.

Looking back, it was really all about survival, going through such a threatening and scary experience, which caused me to feel so much inner panic. The thing is back then the term or words "lost" and "identity" would not have been used, and expressing how you felt emotionally wasn't encouraged.

Going through some of those very distressing emotional times led me to eventually understand and become much clearer that finding myself, my true identity, and loving myself was going to be my life's work. Healing that deep inner love of self, my purpose of assisting and uplifting others, to truly understanding in many ways that you don't need to find yourself, because you are yourself.

Positive lifestyle changes were what began to support my inner strength, putting me in the right direction of embracing that huge lifestyle experience. I was very sensitive, vulnerable and an introvert, again words that wouldn't have been recognised then, and were known more as weaknesses, which I even believed as I allowed others to infringe on me back then.

Not realising or understanding that it was OK to be sensitive, as it really is a strength and the world needs more sensitive people. In fact, these gifts, Sensitivity, Vulnerability and Invisibility, were and still are what has defined me, and to my life unfolding, a witness of my true identity. Once you are aware of how disciplined you are in helping yourself, then you realise you want to help others do the same, by helping themselves as well.

Homeopathy, nutrition and meditation were also key factors to getting me back on track, and was such a positive breakthrough in so many ways, accepting I have this natural positive approach to wanting to help myself; asking and seeking for that help is paramount on your inner healing journey.

Having mental strength, positive thoughts, added a huge part in embracing my beliefs, leading me to really grasp the true meaning of grace, feeling worthy of God's love, realising God's love had always been there, to then understand grace is all of God's spiritual blessings, and one of the most glorious is grace.

But I had forgotten to connect with God and ask for his guidance, choosing to go it alone. The result of feeling lost, not feeling connected spiritually, but to then receiving his gift of grace. It personally felt like God was representing me, helping me to remember to ask for his help, connecting to the higher energy.

"God, I don't want to abuse your grace, God, I need it every day, it's the only thing that makes me want to change."

We The Kingdom

Through grace I was inspired, and influential people started coming into my life. New doors started opening daily, providing me with opportunities to achieve my true potential. Understanding the depth of gratitude and abundance which was constantly flowing to me.

I began to connect and feel that alignment, to then opening to receive, believing in dreams, desires, to feeling deserving.

Grace is everywhere, it truly is Amazing Grace all of the time. Do you need an outpouring of God's grace to help you do what you have been or are being called to do?

"Grace is the Divine in action, surrender to that grace."

You may be thinking how did I get to my place of grace, not feeling lost, and to then finding myself. Unknowingly for many years I had been affected by layers and layers of negativity that were shrouding my existence, all created by me, to causing many of my emotional situations. It took deep transformational work, helping me heal and I surrendered to grace.

Surrendering, releasing, to letting go of control and really reaching out, and once you realise you can't do it alone to asking a higher power/God is when you begin to experience signs of grace seeking to connect with you, as sometimes those experiences are grace trying to get your attention. Surrendering to grace, trusting and knowing you will receive more love into your life.

Then you will begin to see the dark despair that kept you captive for many years, start to diffuse and begin to delete many aspects that no longer serve you. Evolving and helping yourself is when you truly understand that by helping yourself you eventually will help others. Self-care is how you can take back your power, because when you evolve, others around you will too.

Aligning to your divine self is a magical moment, as it opens you up to so much more. Prayer, meditation and other supportive techniques can become your spiritual tools within your daily spiritual practice. Let your spiritual practice stimulate your dreams and visions, providing you with the divine guidance and wisdom to then awaken them into your life.

What you find yourself learning is that your healing heart is ready to receive, to then gratefully balancing all your giving. Grace is from the heart and you begin to feel that powerful thread of love and light, becoming a powerful receiver of divine grace and believing your dreams are truly real.

The Universe is celebrating your commitment of God working in and through you, to blessing the world with more

11

balance. Then the start of something beautiful unfolds as you really begin to embrace all of your gifts that you were born with, to enjoying all the synchronicities that make your life feel more effortless and so "grace-full".

"Never underestimate the power of dreams and the influence of the human spirit. We are all the same in this notion. The potential for greatness lives within each of us."

Wilma Rudolph

"God's got me here for something. I can feel it. I was born for everything that I'm doing now."

Muhammad Ali

I still believe, as insightful as all this is, that there has to be much more meaning to how it can support us in living a peaceful and meaningful life. The benefits that we would feel can be by starting to embrace grace, which will then lead us to practising gratitude, it will then help to find joy in each moment, to becoming a priority and finding a place for grace.

Gratitude is the quality of being thankful, a readiness to show appreciation. So each day you can make it a habit to really feel the feelings of gratitude, think and feel the words "thank you" in your heart.

They are powerful words and the more you use gratitude every day, the more you will transform your life, there are no limits to the good that you will bring forth to yourself. Feel your heart calling you home to love and gratitude, giving thanks for a grateful heart. Therefore, give thanks in all circumstances to fulfil the will of God.

Here are a few verses to repeat often:

"I am grateful that all the wisdom and beauty of the Universe is being expressed through me."

"I am deeply grateful that peace is appearing in my home, in my heart and in all my affairs."

"I am grateful that everything in my life is coming to me effortlessly and easily at all times."

"I am grateful that I am the brilliant conscious creator of my life and therefore all things in my life can be created or changed through my conscious direction."

When I think back to my childhood, the only memories I can remember of the word grace would have been expressing gratitude through saying the prayer of grace before a meal. As a family we would say it together and the words were:

"For what we are about to receive, may the dear Lord make us truly grateful."

I still feel and find it a pleasing thing to say, and at most times I find myself remembering to recite it quietly, it could be before a meal or maybe something that feels like a blessing that I am truly grateful for, because there is always a time and place for grace.

*"Grace isn't a little prayer you chant before receiving a meal.
It's a way to live."*

Jacqueline Winspear

Any negative things that we may experience in life can be encouraged to be always positive when we practise gratitude through grace, as we all have this power within us that is greater than the world.

It is now time to begin thinking and acting in an empowered way. Are you ready to start engaging and using your full power?

To ignite the power of the Universe from within you is to simply start by saying thank you for the ability to love, which knows no limits, and to be in harmony with the power of love and gratitude.

"It is about being at one with the very power that created you."

These words, Grace, Intention, Manifestation, Karma, Responsibility and Unconditional Love are known and explained as the "Law of One".

When you start to know as a person those feelings of love for another in your heart, you will then know that the love will always reach them. Never underestimate love and gratitude, as the saying goes, it can part seas, move mountains and create miracles in your life.

Practising gratitude personally is and has been in my life a while now, and I thank God for my magnificent life, I describe the experience and the feeling daily, which is that I feel the gratitude oozing out of every cell in my body.

"God is the only power and that power is within me. There is only one plan, God's plan, and that plan now comes to pass. I give thanks that I now bring forth from the Universal Substance everything that satisfies all the righteous desires of my heart. The divine of my life now comes to pass."

Florence Scovel Shinn

"For by grace are ye saved through faith, and that not of yourselves; it is the gift of God."

Ephesians 2: 8

"Let us therefore come boldly to the throne of grace that we may obtain mercy and find grace in time of need."

Hebrews 4: 16

Sharing quotes like these from the Bible seems to encapsulate my own personal expression, so I hope you will embrace them, just pause for a moment, read them again, then pop them into your grateful heart.

What does it mean to be saved by grace? With God we have this insurance, it's called grace and it is free, all you have to do is ask and he will help you. He is faithful, faith alone is God's word saying that we are saved by grace through faith in Jesus Christ.

"Faith is a willingness to step into the unknown."

Grace alone means that God loves, forgives and saves us, not because of who we are or what we do, but because of the work of Christ. Grace is sacred and connected to God with the meaning

15

of forgiveness, repentance, regeneration and salvation and is in the Grace of God.

"I am not lucky, I am blessed. Everything I have is because of God's grace and favour. Your Grace is enough, Lord."

Faith has been and is my foundation, it is trusting and believing in God's word, even when you don't always have evidence of things working out. Your faith in God is your life and power.

Spirituality explains my faith, because it is an internal/inward journey of self-discovery, it's less about "doing" and more about "being" our truest most authentic self, and is then everywhere we go.

It truly can be a Sacred Journey, as I really felt I was born a sacred being, although unaware at the time, and being the beginning of my spiritual journey. Trials can become a springboard into an awakening.

I feel I personally came with many lessons to learn, especially the love of self and learning to connect with my soul, understanding my soul to be my true identity.

My spiritual understanding of the love of self is that I am in touch with my divinity, as I believe spirituality is not about religion. Religion to me is external, and my faith showed me it wasn't about religion, I learned that it is a higher knowing, a higher love and that the trust, belief and courage that God bestowed upon me expressed that faith to how I would survive with God's love.

Faith is believing or trusting that all will work out, even if you don't always have evidence, so trust in God's word and keep on believing.

"Now faith is the substance of things hoped for, the evidence of things not seen."

Hebrews 11: 1

Faith is a powerful gift, it also really helped me in my life, where I was to learn that God was my strength and would help me embrace many more gifts, an introvert, empathic, sensitive and vulnerable.

"Faith is a living and unshakable confidence, a belief in the Grace of God."

Martin Luther

Faith eventually inspired me and then, with the help of grace, I felt the strength of my faith to remembering who I truly am. Developing peace of mind, feeling fulfilled to receiving and giving love, truly was that guiding star to allowing the grace of the angels to walk in my everyday functions.

"Faith is the first place where self-esteem begins its journey within us."

Stephen Richards

Personally I have learned to accept many gifts that may have been frowned upon in those times, but these gifts have helped me learn to manage and identify who I am to help the greater cause and make a difference. Understanding that you are receiving gift after gift, all situations, experiences, truly do match a Christian understanding of grace, as the aim is connecting to feel that higher love.

Greatness comes from the desire to do extraordinary things, there is a greatness in all of us, but we must first choose to be great.

"Be not afraid of greatness; some are born great, some achieve greatness, and others have greatness thrust upon them."

William Shakespeare

Your Sacred Journey is a healing process that leads you to that place within, which is the love of God. A powerful love that helps you connect to something sacred and holy, helping you reclaim the love of self, understanding that this power is positive.

"May the Grace of the Lord Jesus Christ, and the love of God, and the fellowship of the Holy Spirit be with you all."

2 Corinthians 13:14

Dr Wayne Dyer also says it is all within you, all the knowledge of the Universe is deep within you. You are connected to all of it, to Source, to God, or whatever you choose to call it. Just go within and become quiet and trust what you find, what you feel and what you know.

"Awaken to the divine intelligence within."

Wayne Dyer

The gift of your saving grace is to breathe in love, compassion and grace.

CHAPTER 2

GRACE

REMEMBER

A SACRED JOURNEY

GRACE

REMEMBER
YOU ARE A RADIANT SPIRIT

A Radiant Spirit you most certainly are, but you need to remember this, your soul wants to dig deeper.

As I continued to write this chapter and realising the title was Remember, two things popped into my head; firstly, my cheeky Spirit was calling me to sing this verse that wanted to roll off the tip of my tongue.

This is the verse: "Remember, remember the fifth of November", oohing and aahing as you look up into the sky and remember why. Of course it was Guy Fawkes Night where the magical fireworks truly do light up the sky.

Then secondly, I realised it was 11 November 2020, and remembering it was Remembrance Day.

This was the day when mainly the British remembered those who died in the two world wars, and you would see many displays of the beautiful red poppies which are now such a part of that memory.

It then made me stop and I found myself thinking of my father, and remembering how much it all meant to him, because that memory would have been so poignant for him too.

He would have remembered his time as a dispatch rider, as he lived with those memories until the day he died, he was always keen to share his stories with us and many others, telling us all about those deep, meaningful and challenging times. How could he not remember!

At his funeral where we celebrated his life, my family and I were able to invite a bugler, a lovely lady who played The Last Post, such a treasured memory and it touched us all deeply.

Also on that day we received the flag bearer from his regiment, so all in all it was understandably a very emotional day, but we had such very special memories too. Memories I will always remember and have in my heart.

Celebrating his life in this way on that day has made me even more aware now each year, to understanding the meaning of Remembrance Day, because they were all heroes of that time.

Even though I have huge respect for the fallen, I am more aware now of wanting to remember and hold memories of many other heroes too. Not only in the past or even recent years, but also the present ones, because I feel all heroes need to be reminded, and most definitely they also need to be remembered as well.

Remembering can mean to bring to mind, or to think of again, and "recall" is to bring back to mind, and recollect, as they are all senses.

Remembering allows you to bring a piece of information back into your mind or to keep a piece of information in your memory. An example could be when you reminisce about those past memories, maybe a holiday or even reciting a poem after hearing its title.

As I continue writing I feel inclined and want to share more memories, some of my personal long-term memories, happy ones that played a big part in my childhood, which happened on my grandparents' farm. It feels important to share, they are lovely positive memories that I remember as if they were only yesterday.

I grew up in a small community where everyone knew each other, helped each other, and, that old cliché that we hear often, we were like one big family.

The farm was only ten minutes away, so most days I would cycle to see my grandparents, helping them when I could. I just loved the farm life, it always made me feel safe and happy being there. Feeding the chickens, collecting the eggs, watching my grandad milk the cows, ploughing the fields. I remember with such fondness Flower the carthorse, and many times I was allowed to sit on her back, holding on to the amazing harness.

Remembering those very special happy memories and really feeling and reliving those precious moments, and feeling blessed.

But one day, Flower the carthorse became very ill from an infection in her hoof and she died. Now this memory nearly makes me cry, as my dear grandad was a very gentle soul and I remember how very upset he was. I was only about 11 years old, but I could see how distressed he was, because I knew the love of his animals meant the world to him.

That sadness stayed with me for a long time, and it was my first time seeing how my grandad experienced such sadness too. His life was the farm, his dedication to all his animals really did mean so much to this very kind and loving man.

But of course I can also remember my brothers and sister on the farm, because we had so many other wonderful experiences, including lots of fun and laughter, which made it very special too.

We all enjoyed the haymaking season, getting involved helping out, as in those days they were very hot summers. I remember the big wooden rakes used in helping to make the bales of hay, and sitting on the tractor was always a treat. Fun and laughter was always the theme of us enjoying ourselves.

The other fun part we all witnessed was my brother learning to drive, and he had been allowed to practise by driving around in the fields, so we all spent loads of time riding round in his old car, he even took the roof off, making it easier for us all to climb in.

We really did have the best times together, very special memories, so writing and remembering them has certainly been one way of bringing them all back, with such gladness and very much still in my heart.

Having been brought up in the countryside was delightful and reminiscing is such a healthy thing to do. I feel so blessed to have had those times in my childhood.

Reminiscing about parts of your life, or any information that you are able to bring back into your mind, is that recall for remembering. Allowing my life to unfold as I continued on my Sacred Journey of remembering.

The next chapter of my life after my childhood in the countryside was to find myself wanting to spend it living by the coast. The countryside was still only a short distance away from the sea, so I had the best of both worlds.

I love the expansiveness and openness of living by the sea, it was and still is where I love being. So sharing the memories really has been instrumental to how I can embrace remembering who I am.

I do think that what is also important to remember is that each person will react differently when they remember, because we can all have good or bad memories. There is a saying that goes: 'She or he remembered who they were, and the game changed'.

Now here's the thing, can you remember who you were before

the world told you who you were? Maybe not, so again keep on remembering who you are, not letting the world, or others who may try to, change you into someone else, just remember not to let them.

Remember at the beginning of this chapter, I wrote: "You are a Radiant Spirit" and that you need to remembers your soul wants to dig deeper.

Radiant spiritual beauty belongs to the one who sees beauty in all things and remember the divine origin of that beauty within... with each breath.

"Beauty may be in the eyes of the beholder, but radiant beauty flows from the heart of the soul."

Radiance is your birthright, a radiant person respects their own feelings, they live life passionately, and this radiance is the one soul wanting to express itself, all its emotions, to following the guidance of their soul, to radiating out beams of light.

So this is a good place to now think about other aspects of this chapter of Remember which is fascinating when you start to think where you came from and otherwise maybe not knowing where you are going.

Remember who you are, keep on remembering, letting God take care of the hows in your life, to then knowing the importance of really remembering who you truly are.

"Remember today, as if it was a play, reminding you who you are, that special, kind and caring soul, playing a very important role. Remember why you are here, coming back to learn so much more, remember like never before."

Quietly, keep reminding yourself of who you really are, as you uncover your true light from many layers of fear, forgetfulness that you actually have allowed to dampen your hope, trust and faith, to then find meaning and purpose, reclaiming your passion for life, unlocking hidden treasures of self-confidence, and that inner peace with self.

Be more yourself, allow and give yourself all the space, time and love you need to remember who you are.

"Don't limit yourself. Many people limit themselves to what they think they can do. You can go as far as your mind lets you. What you believe, remember, you can achieve."

Mary Kay

Have you seen the wonderful musical The Lion King? The great Circle of Life connects all living things. Look inside yourself, you are more than what you have become, remember who you are, remember.

A famous line, taken from an African-American spiritual, is: "Nobody knows the trouble I've seen, nobody knows my sorrow," and as you go through life, you will see that there is so much that we don't understand, and the only thing we know is things don't always go the way we plan. You have forgotten who you are, and so forgotten me.

This would have been Mufasa: "You have forgotten who you are and so have forgotten me. Look inside yourself Simba." And again Mufasa says: "Remember who you are, you are my son, and the one true king."

Simba's father encouraged him to remember who he was and to take place in the Circle of Life. Yes, life does happen, but you can move forward and learn from the past, taking those lessons into becoming who you were always called to be.

So you cannot run or escape from what happens to you, but know that God is always with you in those dark times, because in those dark times it is when you will need to remember who you are, and you can choose to become all that you were created to be. Most importantly always knowing that you have the love, compassion and grace that is in your life. It is that portal of connection to the divine grace, your Source centre, that you feel is your much longed-for home.

Remember your spiritual growth when you worked on your inner self, known as your invisible support system, achieving your outer being, which is to be visible.

Remember your sensitivity, sincerity, awareness, affection and gentle grace, it makes you who you are, so don't give up on the person you're becoming, as regeneration removes many wasted years or opportunities, it would be a process of coming back, a spiritual rebirth, reawakening and feeling rejuvenated, remember you are a spiritual being having a human experience.

Remember, living outside yourself is exhausting, to then

realising how resilient you are and embracing your inner strength, releasing, setting yourself free and letting go of control. There is so much more to you than you have realised, now you are remembering.

Remember God in the dark times as "grace teaches us to let go and let God".

"God does not command that we do great things, only little things with great love."

Mother Teresa

"Whenever you find yourself doubting how far you can go, just remember how far you have come. Remember everything you have faced, all the battles you have won, and all the fears you have overcome, Jesus says, 'repent and believe'."

N. R. Walker

Remember, love generates love, God exists within us all, love conquers all.

"I am remembering my true nature. My true nature is light, my true nature in spaciousness. I remember my true connection to God/Goddess. I am a free Sovereign Being, I am my power, I am my light."

In this time of Ascension, I am called to move beyond all the chaos on the earth plane, and you can raise that power in the best and most beneficial way too. When you remember the presence of grace and staying plugged into it, to remembering always being connected to the Divine.

Be mindful always, as the flow of abundance is truly present in each sacred moment, a state of being safe and sheltered from anything that can make you feel vulnerable. Grace then becomes important for when we really need to remember ourselves as divine, resilient and strong.

Remember that acceptance does not mean approval, you don't have to like reality, but in order to reduce your suffering you do have to accept it.

"May I remember that there is a positive outcome in every situation, when divine love is present."

CHAPTER 3

GRACE

ACCEPTANCE

A SACRED JOURNEY

GRACE

ACCEPTANCE
ACCEPT THE POWER OF LOVE

The laws of Spirit, no matter what one's beliefs are, God's law, is love, and spirituality and religion can all represent a passageway to mental and emotional freedom, and the first law could just be that stepping stone along this path to that freedom, which is acceptance.

The power of love and accepting "what is" and allowing change to happen all around you, but without attachment. These two energies, acceptance and allowance, really do help your Ascension experience, and accepting the Ascension process is divine guidance, as all is in divine perfect order.

"Open, accept and allow all the new aspects of awareness and deeper experiences that are coming into your heart."

Relaxing more, allow the process, and live in that expansion, which is your divine birthright, giving you a broader perspective about life and freedom.

Feeling connected to your Higher Self, bringing you joy and being lovingly aware, will occur in and around you, both personally and globally, as it means to accept what is occurring without judgment. Believing there is a reason for any current experience, helping your growth and expansion to moving forward with greater ease.

When in judgment, "what is" and resisting your present reality can often cause extreme stress in your physical and emotional body. The denser energies are sometimes why you may experience discomfort, either physical or emotional, meaning you could be out of alignment. The resistance and fear can intentionally block your process, and those blocking symptoms could be panic, anxiety and depression.

Usually becoming aware of the stress might finally remind you that your situation can't change for the better until you see that gripping part of you that is in control, because there are so many things that can get in your way.

When you can focus and look at some of those changes that you know will make a difference in your life, it will be about remembering that sometimes your intentions are the answers, really beginning to trust the Universe and understand and learn to accept "what is" Above, create a space of letting go, release and surrender to any outcomes or agendas, to being in that space of neutrality, allowing and accepting it to be a part of your spiritual practice.

A spiritual practice does require acceptance, and allowing is the other key word, they are two of the greatest powers available to you, so then put together, being in alignment with the Source energy, you can take those steps that will enhance you to a new level of ease.

The infinite healing presence within is part of your transformation, so give thanks and know you will be in alignment always.

"I am allowing the infinite intelligence to work through me."

It is about remembering to trust your powerful support system that is built within you, to then apply those steps to get the changes you are looking for in your life. You will achieve a much greater feeling of wellbeing, it truly will encourage you to actually step back and receive the love and support needed, a result of your positive action.

Always remembering to thank God/Source for giving you this awareness and strength that you need in accepting situations in the world that don't always feel right for you.

Repeat: "I am accepting my divine plan," God's plan, so have faith, relax and learn to allow life to really unfold and align you to the light and the higher good for life on earth.

"I accept miracles into my life, I believe in miracles, miracles happen to me."

The flow of life feeling free really can be about letting life unfold, and not getting in the way, or as the saying goes, to get out of your own way. Experiencing acceptance can come to you at any time, and in many situations where you may find yourself experiencing something that has happened, to then thinking OK, I have a choice, I can either say: "I will accept this," or just breathe and let it go and accept.

This affirmation might help:

"I accept the situation as it is right now, even if I don't like it."

So why is accepting yourself unconditionally so difficult? Apparently to help yourself, you need to give up the actual fantasy of punishing yourself enough with so many negative thoughts that you felt would help that change, to thinking you could shape yourself by saying negative things like: "I'm weak when I feel any anxiety," or you might even say: "Why did this have to happen to me?" But it is finding the strength to go towards what is actually in front of you, because that path of acceptance really does work.

This is where recalling a situation in the past that you were able to accept can and will help encourage you to keep practising reality acceptance. The spiritual word for not fighting with reality is acceptance, and the religious word is surrender, as the more you accept, the easier your life can become.

Be assured that acceptance also doesn't mean that you give up or that you stop trying; it doesn't happen overnight because sometimes the more painful the situation, the harder it will be to accept, and it feels it's hardest to then allow and let go of your emotional resistance.

Pain, loss or injustice are inevitable, as they are all part of life's experiences and many situations. It is about understanding the distinction between acceptance and resignation, because accepting emotions doesn't always mean you resign to feeling terrible or wallowing in pain. It could simply mean being aware of your emotions, accepting them for what they are in the moment, knowing they won't last.

Acceptance can free you up to use your energy wisely, rather than deplete it with unhealthy attitudes and endless questions.

For many of us our first impulse is to resist something that we do not like that comes our way, so acceptance requires overriding this impulse and choosing to breathe into and through the experience, trusting that it has value, that is for us and not against us.

The truth of the matter is that resistance prolongs the negative experience, and acceptance allows for the possibility of changing our experiences by changing our attitude.

"The basis for true change is freedom from negativity, and that's what acceptance implies, having no negativity about what is, and then you see what the moment requires; what is it that is required now so that life can express itself more fully."

Eckhart Tolle

41

Acceptance is saying:

"It is what it is and what it is, is what it is."

Eckhart Tolle

Grace can be understood as the virtue of accepting others without being judgmental, as grace, in a practical sense, is involved with a process of maturity. A mature person does not see himself as God in the life of another. The more mature one becomes, the more acceptance will be demonstrated in their life.

Ways to help practise acceptance would be not having mixed judgment, so try to avoid thinking of situations as good or bad and simply see them for what they are. Acknowledge yourself always and be clear, accepting yourself doesn't imply weakness or mean giving up and staying in the same place, as you start with yourself, to finding only the good.

"It is the willingness to let go of your Emotional Opposition, to the reality of 'what is'."

Eckhart Tolle and Byron Katie

"Accept… then act to whatever the present moment contains, accept it as if you had chosen it… this will miraculously transform your whole life."

Eckhart Tolle

When you begin to accept what is and not allow yourself to get discouraged, you can then figure out with a much greater calmness and clarity, remembering that accepting reality will help the intensity of your emotions, to being kind to yourself, but to also keep going.

Be grateful for the awareness you start to experience, a strength to accept situations that do bring you into that alignment, a place of alignment that can assist you to feel inspired. Remembering to ask for what you need, as God does hear your prayers. Then when you trust and allow that change to occur, it will be in accordance with your highest intentions.

Self-acceptance is feelings of satisfaction with one's self, regardless of past behaviours or choices.

"For our present troubles are small and won't last very long. Yet they produce for us a glory that vastly outweighs them and will last forever."

2 Corinthians 4: 17

In my case, I found "accept what is" to be very challenging on my transformational and personal journey. On many different levels you start to accept what is, coming through many situations, to then realising there are other levels still to learn.

When you are a perfectionist and have high ideals, which can really inspire you, filling you up with hope and direction, to then knowing the essence of a true vision is about acceptance.

Sometimes it's realising you do have to come down to earth and actually appreciate the perfection of here and now, to accepting ourselves and others in the present moment. Then acceptance can form that bridge into a more joyous life, to then helping practically and effectively in contributing to the world.

What specific ways can you practise to then bring a much greater acceptance into your life? You could allow yourself and others to evolve to God's pace, and not your own. Your job is to have no attachment to the appearance of disharmony, but to hold to the love within all things.

"Accept what is and allow change to occur around you without attachment."

If you emotionally oppose the path of acceptance, you might find yourself with no choice other than having to turn back and walk its counterpart, being the path of resistance.

The reason more of us are not spiritually aware is that we often don't or won't accept what is happening, to accepting we are spiritual beings having human experiences. When you understand there is so much more to you, then you realise, you are remembering.

It would be a conscious choice to drop all forms of resistance to any given situation that can present itself, and acceptance is not about liking or approving of something, it is usually the flow of consciousness that moves on to the next thing, unfolding and also without you getting in the way.

"When you argue with reality you lose, but only 100% of the time. The first and most important thing is to learn about acceptance, what is and what isn't."

Byron Katie

Acceptance is a conscious choice to drop all forms of resistance to whatever has become present in the moment, to then making the most of it, because it's not about liking or approving of something. But it is about letting life flow and unfold. Being receptive, rather than extending resistance to what becomes present.

You do have to bear in mind that acceptance is not the same as forgiveness. You work on yourself, as it has nothing to do with the other person. Forgiveness is optional, but acceptance is necessary for you to move on with your life.

When you have attained the virtue of acceptance, you can then exercise other virtues too, like awareness, generosity, consideration, flexibility, forgiveness, tolerance, patience and trust.

Serenity is often cited as the grace, the gift that allows acceptance of things that ought to be changed. So accept love, connect with the spiritual aspect of life, that invisible part of going within.

We actually do come into the world as beings, wanting to experience and learn from this life that we have chosen, we choose to come into this time, place, wanting to help bring changes to the earth, as it is that higher level that is needed in life to the awakening of Now.

Getting real about living authentically means uncovering wounds or mistakes and accepting them with grace, including embracing both your strengths and flaws, and in addition not comparing yourself with others, but to seeing yourself as a unique being who is still growing. We have all made mistakes, even survived those mistakes, but mastering acceptance of those past mistakes is your key to emotional freedom.

It could be the alignment with those life lessons and the teachings that are needed to then bring your own life into a higher order, because with a divine purpose that is really supporting you, then you can allow so much more energy to flow through you, connecting to that higher level.

"I align my actions to my life purpose."

Allowing yourself to be who you are, while also understanding how others might see you, as this can help to see whether you are being authentic and true to your inner self. Proof of your acceptance of self is when you are taking the action to empower yourself, when you are truly Sovereign [empowered] choosing to be you.

Ask yourself what peace would it bring to you if you were able to accept yourself just as you are right now, your life as it is now and others as they are.

Grace is the power of prayer, God goes with you wherever you go, God is your strength and vision is his gift.

"God is your Source, God is the light in which I see. God is the mind with which I think. The light has come, I have forgiven the world. GRACE is to let it be."

CHAPTER 4

GRACE

COMPASSION

A SACRED JOURNEY

GRACE

COMPASSION

*"Compassion is a natural gift of kindness for yourself
and others."*

Compassion is such a sacred word, I want you to just stop a
moment... put your hand on your heart, trust and know you
have that connection of pure love, it is a natural state of grace
and abundance, feel yourself being present, to embracing this
beautiful golden sacred moment.

The word compassion brings me into an instant sense
of meditation, calm, peace and total serenity, and when
compassion is practised and felt, it will help you become more
resilient, improving your overall wellbeing.

"It is better in prayer to have a heart without words than words without a heart."

Mahatma Gandi

Compassion is such an extension of love, and we all have it, we just forget it is there. Both love and compassion are two positive feelings that help to make the world a better place. The powerful force of compassion is what every person desires and every human being really does deserve it, so remember to have that compassion towards yourself, dear one… as you are always doing the best you can.

Compassion and communication really do help change lives, because it's about working on opening your heart, going deeper. And as you personally grow and transform yourself, opening your heart, feeling compassion for yourself, of course then you will feel that same compassion also on a deeper level for others.

My own personal transformation led me to realise my life purpose was going to be communication, hence studying and qualifying to become a psychotherapist, life coach and an author. Communication is an important life skill, effective communication has the benefits of helping build trust, relationships and providing clarity and direction. Verbally, it is a language used to transfer information through speaking, and is very effective. Written communication is also effective and I know that writing my books is a very positive way of communicating, and is so rewarding.

"I share my gifts to awaken the world."

Communicating from a place of love really is the way to speak and listen, opening the heart, then the doorway of your communication centre opens up, your throat chakra will give you the ability to express yourself fully, to then hearing others with openness, and increasing more compassion and connection. This approach also helps you say things in a calmer, clearer and caring way.

Consciously you let the positive habit keep leading to even more love, keeping your heart open. That is being authentic, listening without judgment and truly sharing what you are thinking or feeling and empathically hearing and feeling those needs in the words that people are saying. All such wonderful examples of becoming more compassionate.

The temple of the heart is when your heart centre is open. Speaking from love, listening, to then making the decision to become that powerful conduit for love that is within.

Finding the voice of our soul can really begin to help in understanding the different levels that we go through, and why we seem to silence the voice of our soul that is always calm and determined.

But ultimately knowing and leading us to the true meaning of feeling God's presence.

Let your voice express compassion.

"I listen to no other voice than the voice of my soul.

My voice is to show compassion for…

My voice is to speak with love to…

My voice is to connect with others.

My voice is your VOICE."

Having compassion, being kind to yourself, is a strength, expressing gratitude, being mindful and feeling deeply for another person, teaching others, and with a willingness to give.

The Bible defines compassion by showing us what compassion looks like and what is involved with being compassionate.

Cultivating compassion is firstly having that compassion for ourselves, and knowing what is present internally is so essential, because at the centre of your being you have all the answers, you know who you are and you know what you want.

"How can I look after myself in this moment and what can I do to support myself?"

To have the benefits of meditation is helpful, understanding how powerful it is, to also knowing that it helps access the part of your brain which is less reactive and responsible. It simply and certainly helps us learn the strength of compassion and patience.

Of course, to be able to have compassion for others, we then need to develop it within ourselves first. So if, for instance, you are judging yourself harshly, and we all have such behaviours, and then numbing everything out. But such behaviours probably would only help us avoid what is actually going on underneath those layers, to us disconnecting from ourselves.

Caring for your inner needs, and to then give yourself time to process those feelings that are arising within, will then help to trust what is really there for you.

Making you realise your increased sensitivity, spiritual insight and intuition is also about even having more empathy, that higher love, appreciating others' circumstances with that kindness in your heart, knowing the power of equality.

It is that bond that unites all of humanity, it is the greatest gift one human being can share with another. Being kind, forgiving each other, as in Christ, God forgave you.

"The Lord is gracious and righteous, our God is full of compassion."

Psalm 116: 5

What is compassion versus empathy? The Latin root for the word compassion is *pati*, which means "to suffer", and compassion means it originates from *compati*. Literally meaning suffer to then feeling compelled to reduce that suffering. This connection of suffering with another person brings compassion beyond sympathy.

However, compassion is much more than empathy, empathy is an ability to relate to another person's pain as if it's your own.

Empathy, like sympathy, is grounded in emotion and feeling, but empathy doesn't have an active component to it, so it would separate compassion from empathy, sympathy, pity, concern, condolence etc.

The spiritual definition is the spirit of the word compassion, not being concerned with material or physical things, but concerned with the human Spirit, involving acting to alleviate the suffering of others. Allowing compassion to embrace the noblest characteristics of human beings, which all helps us to think of others instead of always focusing on ourselves.

I feel that compassion is about getting involved, feeling inspired to help, because you don't have to be a goody-goody to be seen as wanting to help others. But to have and give the ability to understand someone else's situation is having the willpower and showing your heart is open and full of love.

Having the desire to take action with the intent to improve others' lives is knowing how to communicate through that love. When you connect, and hear from your heart, this is known as compassionate listening, it's about having a listening presence, which is a gift you can give to people, because then they feel heard and loved.

Each of us has an endless supply of compassion and it costs us nothing to share it.

"It is not how much you do, but how much love you put into the doing that matters."

Mother Teresa

"There's an urgency on the planet today. We're living at a time on the earth when our great-great-grandchildren can't afford for us to move too slowly. Every place when we are weak, there is in the mind of God, a blueprint, where we become strong. Every place where we are sick, there is a blueprint in the mind of God where we become healthy."

Marianne Williamson

As I write this book, we are having and experiencing a major shift, which is occurring on the planet right now. It feels like a global release of fear, unfortunately due to living in a mind-dominated world, which is sadly obsessed still around power and control. Worrying does not take away tomorrow's troubles, it takes away today's peace.

Something really needs to give around all the world's problems, but equally for us to stay strong and not to be discouraged. Fortunately coming into 2021, we have entered into a life where we will truly be living from the heart, it's the energy of a very sacred fifth-dimension life, a beautiful awakening which is your Sacred Journey, where you will experience freedom and sovereignty.

"Your sacred heart is ready, it will deeply feel the theme of compassion, winning over to that sacredness."

Let us just pause here a moment for this:

"Prayer for Peace

Thank you Spirit for manifesting peace in our world.

Thank you for teaching me how to be peaceful.

Thank you for the peace I feel inside now, may I live peacefully.

I am at peace, I am at peace, I am at peace, I am at peace,
I am at peace."

José Luis Stevens

What is also prominent in this time is the angelic energy wanting to help and support you. It is about allowing the grace of the angels, God's angels, to work with you in your everyday functions, you will receive the angels' assistance with your messenger work.

Archangel Gabriel helps me with my life purpose in communication and this is an example of asking God:

"Dear Archangel Gabriel, thank you for giving me the courage, focus and motivation to write. Thank you for helping me hear true divine messages that I can express through the written word."

So it's remembering to ask God to send the angels to help, really feeling their sacredness in your compassionate heart, so you can begin sharing your unique sacred love story with grace and with ease.

It is important to have that deep compassion and care for others, as you would for yourself as everyone is special and unique. Being inspired and helping to supply the willpower, wanting to help others, and treating them like equals will provide that respect, and really letting the love flow to everyone in the world.

A golden rule in the Bible also says,

"Do unto others as you would have them do unto you."

Matthew 7: 12

Compassion motivates us to get involved, reaching out to those who may be facing difficult situations, being sensitive to what they are experiencing. You have that care at such a profound level that you are filled with this overwhelming desire to make a difference. It makes you accept responsibility that you never thought you could handle, making you a better person than you could ever dream you could be, making your existence meaningful and worthwhile.

Simplicity, patience and compassion are three great treasures shared from the Tao Te Ching:

"Simple in actions and thoughts. Patient with both friends and enemies, as you agree with the way things are. Compassionate towards yourself, you reconcile all beings in the world."

Lao Tzu

It is important to understand that compassion is more than just an emotion, it is a way of life. People are uplifted, encouraged, wanting to embrace the humanity of others because it's genuine, sincere and comes from the heart. Acknowledging the value of another person, with the desire to make the human experience better, not only for ourselves but also for the good of all.

It is very interesting though how we perceive self-compassion, because unconditional self-love does mean treating yourself the way you would treat a beloved friend.

The Buddhist Pema Chodron, calls it Maitri, it is a Sanskrit word for unconditional friendship with yourself. She says that Maitri is a practice and something you actively cultivate through loving kindness and self-compassion.

Practising self-compassion shows you are taking full responsibility for your actions, also helping with reducing self-criticism and any shame.

When you embrace that higher understanding of self-compassion, your wellbeing will improve, it can help with anxiety, depression and thought suppression. The result: achieving a much better life satisfaction too.

"Do not keep searching for the truth, just let go of your opinions."

Buddha

But at other times there still might be those thoughts of feeling judgmental towards yourself. If you do find you are feeling that way then this fabulous process called the ABC of Self-Love, quoted by Marci Shimoff and Carol Kline, is worth remembering.

Awareness: become aware of any negative feelings you are having towards yourself.

Be with the feeling: allow the experience to be there without expressing it or trying to make it go away. Let it be there without trying to change.

Compassion: bring the same kindness and compassion to yourself for having this feeling as you would bring to a dear friend.

This process would support you in mastering self-compassion, and it would require more acceptance as you enter into a new relationship with yourself. Personal empowerment would be another aspect of the self-love centre, allowing and showing you that a much deeper kindness can and will support your inner self.

Naturally you may even remember and find that in past times you might have been very harsh with yourself, and that any adjustment in finding that deeper compassion for self would be part of that process, achieving that mastery.

Your heart centre becomes much healthier, more balanced, giving you that deeper inner strength, and standing up for yourself in everyday situations. In the past, your doorway to self-love would have been closed, where you would have allowed yourself to keep ending up as a victim in your relationships, or other circumstances, which is quite common.

So many people have looked for love, acceptance, affection and attention all their life, so as you proceed on your personal transformation you can and will come to a point where you can say, "I don't want to be someone else, I love myself just as I am," and actually you do become the person you always wanted to be.

OK, so some might say this ABC process is a miracle, but I now know and truly understand it to be called Surrendering to the Flow and Ease of God's Love and Grace.

Of course then there is also self-forgiveness to consider, but this can be built on self-compassion; it would mean making peace with something you did or maybe didn't do, knowing it had made you feel bad.

Feel those feelings, be kind and encourage yourself instead of always feeling demoralised and inflicting punishment, to always losing hope.

Compassion refuses to be selfish, it is willing to forgive and it accepts people for who they are. Jesus' compassion prompted him to act and mercifully love, heal and rescue.

Mercy and its spiritual meaning is described as a love that responds to human needs [kindness] in an unexpected way, and at its core.

"Kindness in words creates confidence. Kindness in thinking creates profoundness. Kindness in giving creates love."

Lao Tzu

Mercy is forgiveness, as with God anything is possible. The difference between mercy and compassion is the treatment of those in distress. Mercy is the fruit of compassion, it is the gifts given to the suffering by those living out their compassion.

Jesus' very presence in the world is the ultimate act of compassion. We did not deserve his sacrifice, but because of

God's great love, we were treated with mercy and are called to live lives of compassion and mercy.

There is no one kinder than Jesus. When he walked upon this earth he showed us how to be kind to others in a way that goes beyond compassion, to the lepers, the lame and the forgotten.

"Be kind and compassionate to one another, forgiving each other, just as in Christ God forgave you."

Ephesians 4: 32

As I have been writing this chapter on compassion, I found myself thinking back to my childhood again, but wanting to purely remember and understand about the village life, and especially the community that I was brought up in. My natural gift of compassion always inspired me to want to help others, and I was taught to be kind to others, but strangely not necessarily towards myself.

Today's teachings, I feel, are guided more around being much kinder to ourselves, loving ourselves as we do unto others. I would definitely say it has been my life's work to do just that, which I feel I can now proudly say is beginning to shine through.

But what does get my attention is how, sadly, the community side of life in today's world has in many ways disappeared. There is still that old cliché of being part of one big family, and the community that I was familiar with and brought up in would have been known as a Christian community.

But now it seems more important to understand that it wasn't just about religion, it was so much more, especially the spiritual aspect, people were very kind and caring and they supported each other.

It was the way of Jesus because he is spiritual, it's not about being religious, he was kind, caring and loving. I now know and believe this to be true, really understanding this, because that's what we felt in our community, it was something that was very natural.

My mum had always been very involved in all the activities in the village and the church, she played a big part in the village community, so we were naturally part of whatever went on. Everyone seemed friendlier then than maybe in the world today.

Then life became so different in many ways and my words would be disconnected, which can give you that feeling of being lost, off-track. My experience was that you do become disconnected from God, and when I was living in the village community, which would have been my bubble, perhaps I took God for granted.

Luckily, the blessing of the Christ Consciousness energy is returning into our lives and the world.

Here is a prayer for compassion and humility.

"Compassion and Humility

Almighty God, we pray for compassion and humility in our hearts. Let us be kind, gentle, generous, loving, giving and forgiving wherever we may go. Allow pride to never get the better of us as you fulfil our dreams. Help us not to have a boastful tongue against our brothers. Let humility invade our souls."

CHAPTER 5

GRACE

ETERNAL

A SACRED JOURNEY

GRACE

ETERNAL

"I am eternally grateful."

This a saying that we would be most familiar with, it exists forever without end. Maybe understanding also that it's lasting, and an everlasting life.

Something that is eternal is the eternal God, and theologically eternal means not within any time limit and outside of time, and existing without a beginning or an end, like Spirit it is used to refer to an everlasting or universal Spirit, represented by God [without beginning or end, lasting forever, always an existing eternal life].

"God is a loving, intelligent and conscious energy."
Bernie S. Siegel

So what is eternal life? Some may say eternal, but what they really mean is everlasting. It's only in this way that God could be everything we think of him, both everlasting and all-knowing.

"God gave us eternal life, and this life is in his Son.
Whoever has the Son has life; whoever does not have the Son of
God does not have life.
I write these things to you who believe in the name of the Son of
God, so that you may know that you have eternal life."

1 John 5: 11-13

Eternal, endless, everlasting, constantly can mean lasting or going on without ceasing. Eternal is by its nature God the eternal Father, that which is endless and never stops, but goes on continuously as in a circle, maybe like the Circle of Life.

"When we die our bodies become the grass, and the antelope eat
the grass, and so we are all connected in the great Circle of Life."

Mufasa (The Lion King)

This life journey on earth is temporary, so eventually our time here becomes complete, but the Spirit does not die, it lives on. We are spirit, we are human and God with all his infinite wisdom gives his Holy Spirit freely to dwell inside those who ask to receive it, making way for his presence to find its home in the innermost sacred space of our hearts.

The Bible tells us everyone will exist eternally, but it is the quality of existence that separates us.

God seriously wants you to take care of your body, because it is where Spirit abides. The same way you strive to take care of your home, God wants you to take care of your body – his home. His desire would be for every believer to really consider the body to be his dwelling place.

Eating nourishing foods, getting enough rest and, most of all, resisting the temptation to do any harm to it. Being mindful too as you go about each day, as God has given your physical being to you for your life purpose.

Are you ready to take care of it in the best way you can, to allow his Holy Spirit to assist you as needed?

My personal transformation over the last two decades at least has guided and led me to understand that God's Spirit resides in me always.

We are physically only born once, but the soul's experiences are an eternal never-ending rebirth, a constant cycle of renewal.

"Don't you realise that your body is the temple of the Holy Spirit, who lives in you and was given to you by God?"

1 Corinthians 6: 19

Eternal life traditionally refers to continued life after death. It includes both the ideas of quality and quantity of life. Eternal life is not simply a life that never ends, but a fullness of life that is unending.

In fact, in many ways eternal life has nothing to do with time, as it can be experienced apart from time as well as within time. It is said to mean unending but it also focuses on the quality or characteristics of that which is eternal.

In scriptures eternal life is strongly connected with Jesus Christ, it is only through him that we experience and receive eternal life.

"And this is Life eternal, that they might know thee, the only true God, and Jesus Christ whom thou hast sent."

John 17: 3

The Bible makes it clear that to know God, you must know the son, Jesus Christ, confessing your disinterest, rebellion or disagreement with God [sin] and then accepting God's arrangement for your salvation.

So to have this eternal life with God, knowing Jesus, scripture says:

"Everyone who believes in him will not be put to shame; for there is no distinction between Jew and Greek; for the same Lord is Lord of all, bestowing his riches on all who call on him. For everyone who calls on the name of the Lord will be saved."

Romans 10: 11-13

"When we believe Jesus came to earth to live a sinless life, rise from the dead, believing you are saved."

Acts 16: 31

"And this is the testimony, that God gave us eternal life, and this life is in his Son. Whoever has the Son has life; whoever does not have the Son of God does not have life."

1 John 5: 11-12

Having belief in Jesus isn't just intellectual knowledge, but I would say a much more personal and faith-based reliance, it is truly about having that relationship with God.

God is invisible, all things were created, things in Heaven and on earth, visible and invisible, and:

"Christ is the visible image of the invisible God."

Colossians 1: 15

To creating this new understanding of who God is, that time is now, where we will all be creating together as the days of this new spirituality are really here and it is time to listen to the voice of your soul.

There are many people awakening, embarking on a time where humanity is remembering, remembering that as an eternal soul and doing what's planned to do on earth. The alignment that you achieve and create from a healthy connection to the nurturing energy of the earth, allowing you to create a strong foundation.

Focusing on spiritual discernment is also important in these times for awakening souls who are discerning helpers. Having and using discernment is eternal wisdom in eternity.

Here is a prayer for discernment:

"We will trust you for generous wisdom, straight paths and peaceful hearts, in all of your glory. How we praise you for being the decision-making God. It's not our decisions but yours that make all the difference. We will plan, but we trust you to order our steps."

"If I only listened to my own rhythm, and tried to live in accordance with it. Much of what I do is mere imitation, springs from a sense of duty or from preconceived notions of how people should behave. The only certainties about what is right and wrong are those that spring from sources deep inside oneself."

Etty Hillesum

We are here to actually see what's here to be seen. Hear what's here to be heard. Taste what's here to be tasted. Smell what's here to be smelled. Touch what's here to be touched. And know what's here to be known…

"There's no great mystery to it. There's nothing magical or mysterious or airy-fairy or even spiritual about it in the way that people usually use the word spiritual…"

Jon Kabat-Zinn

We come to this earth to remember who we are, for insight and self-realisation. Becoming who we truly are is our biggest assignment in life, finding the silence within us. It is inside this silence where we find our true nature. Truly connecting with this silence… this is spirituality. Being spiritual means being no more and no less than just yourself. We are not on earth to become something special, but to become ourselves.

In Neale Donald Walsch's book, *What God Wants*, he mentions that you will begin to understand that death does not exist, but you will know and have that opportunity to learn and to grow, as the process of continuous and unending growth, expansion, self-expression, self-creation and true self-fulfilment unfolds.

"Fear does not stop death, it stops life."

There is a glorious shifting in the experience of the soul, a change in our level of consciousness, freedom, pain release and awareness to the expansion, all leading to a breakthrough in the eternal process of evolution.

A wonderful result for many from this teaching will be to know that death is not to be feared, but part of the wonderful experience called life itself. The Greek word for life [*zoe*] means "God kind of life" which also indicates not only a biological existence but a fullness or genuineness too, and Jesus says he really did come to give us that "God kind of life".

To know that life in one's present physical form is a wondrous gift, understanding at a much deeper level that it may be used to experience who we really are, as your being is eternal.

Imagine the freedom of soul, mind and body that you will experience when at last you understand that you really are one with God. The power that you begin to embrace, to creating a life of your dreams, helping others to also create theirs.

Those frustrations, anxieties, worries all coming to an end. Beginning to realise and believe that all things can be perfect just as they are, because God does not require anything different from you, except you being, doing and having exactly what you are right now.

Such awe and the wonder of life will be expressed by you, enjoying the beautiful expanded awareness you have connected to.

A taste of what life will really be like in this awakened spirituality. Everyone can create it individually to experience it for themselves.

"Every day I strive to get to a place where I'm not affected by the external world, and I don't use the external world to define or tell me who I am. I strive for a state of equanimity, calm and a state of grace, so I can be free of definitions. If you are free, then you can create beautiful things, It's really just shutting out the noise."

Laurel Holloman

We hold the keys to the equation of eternity within our very minds. Once you come to the realisation that we are a precious part of the Universe, a state of inner equanimity is reached. Especially its calmness and composure in difficult times, accepting the good and bad with the balance of equanimity.

"With equanimity, you can deal with situations with calm and reason, while keeping your inner happiness."

The Dalai Lama

Life will invite you to touch those lives, because this is what God is calling you to do right now.

"And the Lord God of all grace called you unto his eternal glory by Jesus Christ, after that ye have suffered a while, make you perfect, stable and strengthened."

1Peter 5: 10

Love is the grace of the sacred gift of purity. God's sacred divinity, the sacred safety of eternity. The sacredness of moments that it shows you as family, aligning the truth.

In your eternal home, you know too that life on earth is but a mirror that shows you to yourself. The beauty, magnificence and sacredness you see in life are a reflection of your own.

I surrender to God asking that he continues to help me align to my true magnificence.

You are that magnificence... You are that sacredness.

An ending prayer:

"A Prayer to Know Your Grace in My Life

Help me O God, because like all men, I need your daily grace. Yesterday's blessings can encourage but will not take care of the burdens of today.

May I know thee as the shepherd of my life and eternal soul. May my fears be dissolved by faith in thee and through the power of thy love.

Help me to love and manifest the spirit of love under all circumstances to all people. May my life be a glory to thyself, a help to my fellow man and rewarding to me.

In Jesus' name.

Amen."

GRACE

MOMENTS OF REFLECTION

A SACRED JOURNEY

Grace

AFTERWORD
Moments of Reflection

Reading this book would have been a commitment you decided to make and experience. Feeling a connection with a positive view of wanting to enhance your life. I feel what I have shared in this book is full of hope, and it is enough.

In many magical ways I hope it will help you know that you are enough too, also wanting to help improve the world as a whole. You have that peace within, so envision a world of peace and plenty, feel the harmony and unity between nations, and contribute to that harmony.

Because you are remembering you came here to this planet to fulfil a very powerful mission, you are no longer a slave to fear, you are a child of God who has sent his Spirit to empower you.

If you feel you are living in any fear, know that God did not give you that fear. God has given us three things: the Spirits of power, love and sound minds.

So, in Jesus' name, say to that fear: "Fear, depart from me for I have the Spirit of power, love and a sound mind," and continue repeating it, saying it until you see and feel that fear depart.

"Let this mind be in you, which was also in Christ Jesus."

Philippians 2: 5

Now walk your path, one that you are meant to walk, and keep sharing your wonderful gifts to help awaken the world.

Remember to keep asking God for his help, receiving the gift of grace, connecting to the higher energy, and embrace the comfort he brings to you as you continue to enjoy the gift of life. So keep praying, believing and embrace the faith.

God only gives three answers to prayer:

1. Yes.
2. Not yet.
3. I have something better in mind.

Reading the Introduction, The Trilogy: GRACE – A Sacred Journey, reading it to the end, hoping that you have found something to inspire and help you, to understand more about the connection with the higher aspect of yourself. A higher love where you experience and feel that alignment, beginning to really start to feel the peace that is within you and to know that you can have grace with ease in your life.

So my prayers are for you, that these five chapters of *GRACE – A Sacred Journey* will support your own unique Sacred Journey. Feeling the love, compassion and grace, helping you from a deeper level where you can and will benefit from your own spiritual awakening.

Enjoy your magical transformation as you continue on your wonderful healing experience as an Earth Angel, connecting with your true powerful inner world, becoming one with the essence of grace, because you are a blessing to the world.

"God's Blessing

Thank you for the world so sweet.

Thank you for the food we eat.

Thank you for the birds that sing.

THANK YOU GOD FOR EVERYTHING."

CLOSING PRAYER

The Praying Hands

*The praying hands are much, much more than just a work of art.
They are the soul's creation of a deeply thankful heart.*

*They are a real expression to God of sincere praise, acknowledging
his goodness in oh so many ways.*

*For when we as his children turn to God in prayer, he never will
forsake us. He'll show his love and care.*

*And in that quiet moment we'll know that inner peace that God
alone can give us, where earthly worries cease.*

John B Knight

ABOUT THE AUTHOR

Dawn is a Transformational Spiritual Author/Healer. She is a charismatic and compassionate soul and her zest and passion for life is infectious.

The three magical words that describe her are inspirational, uplifting and passionate, words that will continue to support her life purpose in communication.

Allowing the voice of her soul to truly co-create with the Divine. Her divine inner light continues to shine brightly, as a messenger of God's love.

A powerful spiritual leader, embracing the connection of the Christ Consciousness. Guiding all souls from that deep place in her heart and soul, helping them to understand their own true meaning of their Sacred Journey of the soul.

Always encouraging others to explore their own uniqueness and feeling the presence of God's love, as it is a powerful and beautiful experience from the Grace of God.

Dawn loves sharing the good news of the Gospel, bringing joy and love to the world.

Contact Dawn: dawnaurora@hotmail.co.uk
www.spiritofdawn.com